The Confessions of St Augustine
Copyright © Frances Lincoln Limited 2001
Text copyright © Caroline White
All illustrations reproduced by kind permission of The British Library
© The British Library Board 2001

First published in Great Britain in 2001 by Frances Lincoln Limited,
4 Torriano Mews, Torriano Avenue, London NW5 2RZ

British Library cataloguing in publication data available on request.

ISBN 978-1-58617-223-7

Set in Baker Signet

Printed in Singapore

1 2 3 4 5 6 7 8 9

Bill Welch
2011

The
Confessions
of
St Augustine

EXTRACTS SELECTED AND TRANSLATED BY
CAROLINNE WHITE

ILLUSTRATED WITH ILLUMINATED MANUSCRIPTS FROM
THE BRITISH LIBRARY

IGNATIUS PRESS   SAN FRANCISCO

dedicated to

parentibus meis

CONTENTS

INTRODUCTION

The *Confessions* of Saint Augustine is a work of great beauty, richness and psychological perceptiveness. Written in the last three years of the fourth century when Augustine was in his mid-forties, its thirteen books are a retrospective account of the author's often troubled journey through childhood, adolescence and early adulthood. Augustine's search for meaning in his life is frankly explored in a manner which is both self-critical and humane, and is of universal relevance. Presented in the form of an address to God, it culminates ultimately in Augustine's dramatic conversion and a decision to commit himself completely to a Christian life.

Although the *Confessions* contains a certain amount of autobiographical detail, it is primarily an investigation into the nature of God and of the human soul, and the relationship between them. Augustine's intention was to explore – and to demonstrate to others – how God had subtly intervened in his life and brought him to the true faith. Reviewing his earlier life, Augustine perceives his spiritual and intellectual development as being made in response to his own dissatisfaction with his way of life at the time. With hindsight, he feels that God was always guiding him, albeit often against his will, towards the divine.

Augustine chose the title *Confessions* for this work not, as is often assumed, merely as a reference to his pre-conversion sins. Although it is certainly true that he spends some time considering the act of theft he committed as an adolescent (p.23 and p.25) and dwells at length on his sexual appetites, the term *Confessions* implies not only a confession of sin but also a confession of praise, and is a powerful expression of Augustine's conviction – attained only after years of painful spiritual and intellectual struggle – that true fulfilment in human life must be centred on God.

In the first nine books of the *Confessions* Augustine reflects on his life up until the period shortly after his conversion, some ten years prior to writing. He was born in 354 to a Christian mother and a non-Christian father in what is now Algeria, but which was then part of the Roman Empire. After completing his education, he taught for a time in his home town and then in Carthage. By this time he had experienced the pleasures of friendship and sex and had a long-term concubine, with whom he had a son. On becoming dissatisfied with teaching conditions in Carthage, Augustine later moved to Rome, accompanied by his concubine and son and followed by his mother, whose deep concern for her son's spiritual state was a profound influence on Augustine – and no doubt an occasional source of irritation.

In 384, however, Augustine moved on from Rome to Milan, where the Emperor's court was based, to take up an important position as Professor of Rhetoric. It was here that he came under the influence of Ambrose, the Bishop of Milan, famed for taking a tough line against non-Christians. Ambrose was also renowned for his skills as a preacher, and Augustine was duly impressed not only by the style of his sermons but also by his ability to reveal the spiritual meaning underlying the Scriptures. Ambrose's teaching came at a crucial moment in Augustine's spiritual development and helped him on his journey towards conversion, which took place in a garden in Milan in the summer of 386 (pp.66–8). Thus committed to God, Augustine renounced all possibility of marriage, family life or any sexual relationship, abandoned his career, and was baptized by Ambrose at Easter 387. Shortly afterwards he began his return journey to North Africa via Rome.

His stay in Rome and his mother's death there are the last actual events recorded in the *Confessions*, but we know that Augustine, at the age of thirty-four, did indeed return to North Africa and remained there until his death in 430. His original intention was to lead a contemplative life of study and prayer with a group of like-minded friends such as Alypius, who had shared Augustine's experience of conversion (p.68). In the months after conversion he had already started writing on philosophy, theology, and the liberal arts and he was to continue to write throughout his life, leaving behind hundreds of works. His prolific output is astounding considering that his desire for a quiet life was thwarted within a few years of returning to his home town, when he was ordained as a priest in the service of the nearby town of Hippo. Augustine eventually became Bishop of Hippo in about 395, and remained in this post for the next thirty-five years.

Apart from giving us information on his career, family and friends, the first nine books of the *Confessions* also provide an insight into the intellectual and spiritual influences that shaped Augustine's thoughts as he moved towards the point of conversion. Although his mother was a Christian, Augustine seems to have had little contact with the Bible: when he did dip into it he found it off-putting both in style and content. Instead, during his teenage years and his twenties his most important influences came from his reading of Cicero's *Hortensius* (a work, now lost, in which Cicero encourages the reader to study philosophy and strive towards immortal wisdom) and his contact with Manichaeism and Neoplatonism, as we see from books 3 to 7.

The Manichees were a Christian sect, founded by the Babylonian Mani in the third century, which had developed a complicated cosmogony based on a belief in two controlling principles, one good and one evil. Augustine seems to have been attracted to this popular sect because of their ascetic and disciplined lifestyle and by what he initially thought was their intellectually sophisticated view of the world and the problem of evil.

However, after about nine years of adherence to Manichaeism, he became disenchanted by their pseudo-scientific explanations and began to look elsewhere for an answer to the problem of evil and the nature of God. When he eventually came across some Neoplatonic writings he was overwhelmed by the plausibility of their world view, in which the universe is regarded as eternal and God is a transcendent, non-material being. Augustine found himself excited by the similarities between Neoplatonism and what he knew of Christianity, and was persuaded by the Neoplatonic belief in evil as a lack of goodness and as a necessary part of the harmony of the universe. He was also attracted by the idea, developed by Plotinus, of the need for the human soul to return to God by means of an intellectual ascent, gradually moving away from the imperfect material realm which drags the soul down, towards the eternal realm which is its true home. As we see from Augustine's account in books 7 and 9 of the *Confessions*, he was able, on brief occasions, to experience such an ascent towards God through the depths of his own soul (p.44 and pp.71–2).

Unlike Plotinus, however, Augustine believed that it was not possible for the human intellect to reach God solely through its own efforts. In Augustine's view divine grace was also necessary. He recognized, too, the need for humility as he saw it exemplified, not only in the life of Christ, but also in the life of Saint Antony, the desert hermit whose biography had such a profound influence on Augustine. The example of Antony as retold by Augustine's acquaintance in Milan, Ponticianus (p.55 and pp.56–8), inspired Augustine with an enthusiasm for the religious life that allowed him to free himself at last from the chains of ambition and sexual desire which were holding him back from a commitment to the Christian faith.

Despite the author's personal convictions and his sophisticated prose style, rich in biblical allusion, the *Confessions* is a very accessible text. Augustine does not overwhelm the reader with dogmatic answers but sets out a perceptive exploration of human psychology and a humane understanding of the anguish involved in our search for happiness. True satisfaction, Augustine believes, can only be found in God, not in a consumer society obsessed with career success and sex, attractive as he admits these things to be. He encourages us to see life as a pilgrimage and to aim towards the future realization of a permanent vision of God; he also portrays life as a continual striving upwards towards the spiritual, away from the excessive and empty enjoyments of the material world.

Augustine's view of the relation between the human soul and God is exquisitely summarized in the following extract from book 10:

So late did I love you, beauty so ancient and so new, so late did I love you! See, you were within me and I was in the external world, looking for you there. In my ugly state I rushed headlong towards those lovely things which you had created. You were with me, and I was not with you. Those lovely things kept me far from you, though if they did not exist in you, then they did not exist at all. You called, you shouted, you shattered my deafness; you shone with dazzling light and dispelled my blindness; you were fragrant and I breathed in deeply and now I am breathless with longing for you. I tasted you and now I hunger and thirst for you; you touched me and now I burn with desire for the peace that is yours. (10:27,38)

IN SEARCH OF GOD

You are great, O Lord, and very worthy of praise; mighty is your power and your wisdom is immeasurable. And mankind, which is part of your creation, wishes to praise you; we who bear the burden of mortality, who carry it around as a testimony to our own sin and to your opposition to the proud. And yet still we wish to praise you, we who are part of your creation. You rouse us to take delight in praising you, because you have made us for your own and our hearts are restless until they rest in you.

Grant me, O Lord, to know and understand whether we should begin by calling upon you or by praising you; and whether we must know you before calling upon you. But who can call upon you without knowing you? For those who do not know you may pray for something that is not you. Or should we rather pray to you in order to learn to know you? But how will people call upon you if they do not believe in you? And how will they believe in you without someone to preach the Word? Those who seek the Lord will praise him, for they who seek him will find him, and when they find the Lord they can but praise him. Let me seek you, Lord, by calling upon you; and let me call upon you when I believe in you; for the news of you has been preached to us. It is my faith that calls upon you, Lord, which you granted me, which you breathed into me through the incarnation of your Son, through the ministry of your preacher. (I:1,1)

WHO ARE YOU, MY GOD?

What then are you, my God? What, I ask, but the Lord God? For who is the Lord apart from the Lord, and who is God apart from our God? You are our absolute, the ultimate good, the most powerful and omnipotent, the most merciful and most just, deeply hidden and yet intimately present, most beautiful and most strong, firmly fixed and yet out of reach, immutable and yet changing everything, never new nor old, yet renewing all things and leading the proud unaware into the weakness of age.

You are always active, always at rest, holding all together but not out of need, supporting and filling and protecting, creating and nourishing and perfecting. You seek although you lack nothing; you love without burning; you feel jealousy without emotion; you grieve but do not suffer pain; you are angry and yet always calm. You change what you have made but you do not change your mind; you rejoice in what you find although it was never lost to you; you are never in need and yet you delight in gain; you are never greedy and yet you demand more. We pay you more than is required so that you will be indebted to us, and yet who has anything that does not belong to

you? You pay off debts although you owe nothing to anyone, and you cancel debts without incurring any loss. But what have I said with these words, my God, my life, my holy sweetness? What does anyone achieve with their words when they speak about you? Yet woe to those who are silent about you for, despite all their chatter, they say nothing of value.

Who will allow me to find rest in you? Who will help me to let you enter my heart and intoxicate me so that I can forget my misfortunes and embrace my one and only good, yourself? What are you to me? Have mercy on me so that I might ask this. What am I to you that you order me to love you and, if I do not, are angry and threaten me with great misery? If I do not love you, then surely that is not a little misery? Alas, in your mercy, Lord God, tell me what you are to me! Speak to my soul and tell me that you are my salvation. (I:4,4–I:5,5)

CHILDHOOD SINS AND VIRTUES

When I was a boy I behaved shamefully, telling countless lies in order to deceive the slave who took me to school and my teachers and my parents. I also used to steal from my parents' cellar and pocket food from their table, either to satisfy my own gluttony or so that I would be able to bribe my friends into letting me win our games, even though they took as much pleasure in playing them as I did. At other times, I won simply by cheating, overwhelmed by my foolish desire to be the winner. Surely I was doing to others exactly what I hated being done to me? I exhibited exactly the same behaviour that I would denounce fiercely when I detected it in others. Yet if I was ever caught out myself and denounced, I would prefer to bluster my way out of it than admit I was at fault.

Is this childish innocence? No, Lord, it is not. And yet, I must thank you, my God, most excellent and supremely good creator and governor of the universe, even if I had not been destined to survive beyond childhood. For at that time I was alive, I could think and I was concerned with self-preservation – a mark of your most profound unity from which I took my being. In my inner consciousness, I protected my mental integrity and took pleasure in the truth even while entertaining petty thoughts about trivial matters. I hated to be deceived, I developed a good memory, I was taught to speak with eloquence, I found delight in friendship, I avoided pain,

despondency and ignorance. What was not admirable and praiseworthy in such a person?

Yet all these qualities are gifts from my God — I did not give them to myself. They are good things and all of them together constitute the person I am. And so he who made me is good, and he is my good, and I shout to him with joy for all the good things that I was even as a boy. My sin lay in seeking pleasure, high ideals and truth not in God, but rather in his creatures — in myself and others. It was because of this that I was plunged into unhappiness, confusion and error. I give thanks to you, my sweetness, my honour and my trust, my God, for your gifts. Please keep them safe for me. In this way you will keep me safe and what you have given to me will increase and be made perfect; I will be with you because you have given me my very existence. (1:19,30–1:20,31)

THE TURMOIL OF ADOLESCENCE

I want to think about my past loathsomeness and the carnal corruption of my soul, not because I love these things but so that I might love you, my God. Out of love for your love, I shall taste the bitterness of remorse and remember my vile ways, so that you may be sweet to me with a sweetness that is not deceptive but pleasurable and lasting. You brought me back from exile where I was in a state of pointless dissolution, for I had turned away from unity in you and become lost in multiplicity.

For a time during adolescence I burned to find satisfaction in hellish pleasures and I dared to run wild amid all kinds of shady passions. My true self wasted away; I became rotten in your sight as I indulged myself and sought to be attractive in human eyes.

What gave me pleasure except to love and be loved? But my relationships went beyond the exchange of minds which marks the bright boundaries of friendship. The eruptions of puberty, like mists rising up from the muddy swamps of my carnal desire, clouded my heart and made it dark until, finally, I could not perceive the difference between the brightness of love and the murkiness of lust: both feelings swirled turbulently inside me, sweeping my youthful

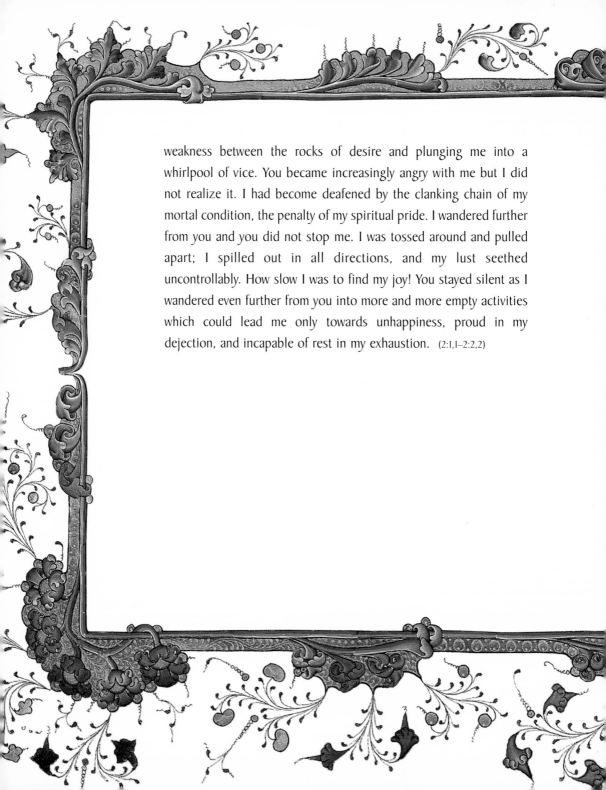

weakness between the rocks of desire and plunging me into a whirlpool of vice. You became increasingly angry with me but I did not realize it. I had become deafened by the clanking chain of my mortal condition, the penalty of my spiritual pride. I wandered further from you and you did not stop me. I was tossed around and pulled apart; I spilled out in all directions, and my lust seethed uncontrollably. How slow I was to find my joy! You stayed silent as I wandered even further from you into more and more empty activities which could lead me only towards unhappiness, proud in my dejection, and incapable of rest in my exhaustion. (2:1,1–2:2,2)

THE THEFT OF PEARS

Keen for me to amuse myself, my parents relaxed the reins as I grew older. But without any strict restraints, I became morally lax and prey to many different emotions. I wanted to commit a theft and I did so, compelled by no other need than a lack of justice and a distaste for it, preferring as I did the rich food of delinquency. I stole something which I already had in plenty and, indeed, of superior quality. My enjoyment lay not in the thing I planned to steal but in the sin of the theft itself.

There was a pear tree near our vineyard which was laden with fruit, although tempting neither in appearance nor taste. At the dead of night, a gang of wild boys (of which I was one) broke from our usual destructive games in the street and headed to the tree to shake down its fruit and steal it. We came away with great loads of pears, not to feast on ourselves but to throw to the pigs. Even if we did eat a few, it was only because we relished doing what was forbidden. (2:3,8–2:4,9)

MY ACT OF THEFT

Contemptible as I was, what was it that I loved in you, my act of theft, that crime I committed one night in my sixteenth year? Since you are a theft, there is nothing beautiful about you – in fact, I am not sure you exist at all for me to address you. The fruit we stole was beautiful because it was your creation, bountiful God. That fruit was beautiful but it was not what my wretched soul desired, for I already had more than enough fruit of better quality. I picked those pears with the sole purpose of stealing them. I threw them away as soon as I had picked them, and feasted only on a wickedness which I took pleasure in savouring. If any of those pears passed my lips, it was the crime that gave them their sweetness. So now, Lord my God, I ask you what it was about the theft that gave me pleasure, for I can see no loveliness in it. It had nothing of the beauty of justice and wisdom, not even that of the human mind – of memory or the senses or physical vitality; nor the beauty of the stars, perfect as they are in their constellations; nor the beauty of the earth and sea, replete with newborn creatures which take the place of those that die. It lacked even that flawed reflection of beauty which makes some vices enticing. (2:6,12)

EVEN IN SIN WE SEEK GOODNESS

Pride, for example, assumes a kind of superiority, but it is false, for you alone are God most high above all things. What does ambition strive for except honour and glory? Yet you alone are to be honoured and glorified above all for eternity. The cruelty of powerful people strives to create fear, but who is to be feared except God alone? What can be taken away or stolen from your power? When or where or how or by whom? Sexual caresses are intended to arouse love, but there are no softer caresses than yours and no object of love is more beneficial than your truth, which is more beautiful and radiant than all other things. Curiosity may appear to be a desire for knowledge, but it is you who know completely. Ignorance, too, and stupidity are flattered with the terms 'simplicity' and 'innocence', yet the greatest simplicity and the greatest innocence lies in you; and dishonest men bring about their own misfortune. Laziness poses as a desire for rest, but there can be no rest except in the Lord. Indulgence likes to be called contentment and plenty, but it is you who are contentment and an unfailing abundance of pleasure that is never corrupted. Extravagance disguises itself as generosity, but you are the most generous bestower of all good things. Avarice is greedy to possess, yet you

possess everything. Envy incites disputes about who is pre-eminent, but what is there more pre-eminent than you? Fear, attendant to its own security, shudders at anything unexpected or strange that might attack what it loves, but to you there is nothing unexpected or unknown. Who can separate you from what you love? And where is there reliable security except in you? Regret pines for the loss of things in which desire took pleasure, wishing that nothing be taken away from it, just as nothing can be taken from you.

So the soul fornicates when it turns from you and seeks what is pure and unadulterated elsewhere, yet its search is futile while it is away from you. All those who place great distances between themselves and you and exalt themselves against you are striving to emulate you, although their attempts are misguided. For even as they imitate you in this way, they are acknowledging that you are the creator of all nature, and so concede that there is nowhere we can truly hide from you.

(2:6,13–2:6,14)

IN LOVE WITH LOVE

I came to Carthage and found myself in a cauldron sizzling with illicit passions. As yet I had never been in love and I longed to be; and in my spiritual emptiness I hated the thought of how I might be if the void were filled. Being in love with love, I looked for an object for my love, and I despised the idea of certainty and a life without risks. I refused to satisfy my internal hunger with your spiritual food, my God, and I was unaware of any need. I had no appetite for incorruptible nourishment, not because I had eaten enough but because the emptier I became, the more unappetizing such food seemed to me. My soul was sick and covered in sores, and it rubbed up against material things in a desperate attempt to relieve the itching. But since material things have no soul, they cannot be loved. To love and also be loved in return was what excited me, especially if I could enjoy my lover's body. So I polluted the stream of friendship with the filth of lust and obscured its brightness with foul passions. But despite this shameful and degrading behaviour, in my excessive vanity I hoped to be regarded as elegant and civilized. I also fell in love – in truth, I was longing to become love's prisoner. My God, how merciful you were, how kind, to mix so much bitterness in with that sweetness: my love was returned and secretly I became enslaved by my joy, happy to be bound by chains, with the result that I was flogged with the red-hot metal rods of jealousy, suspicion, fear, anger and division. (3:1,1)

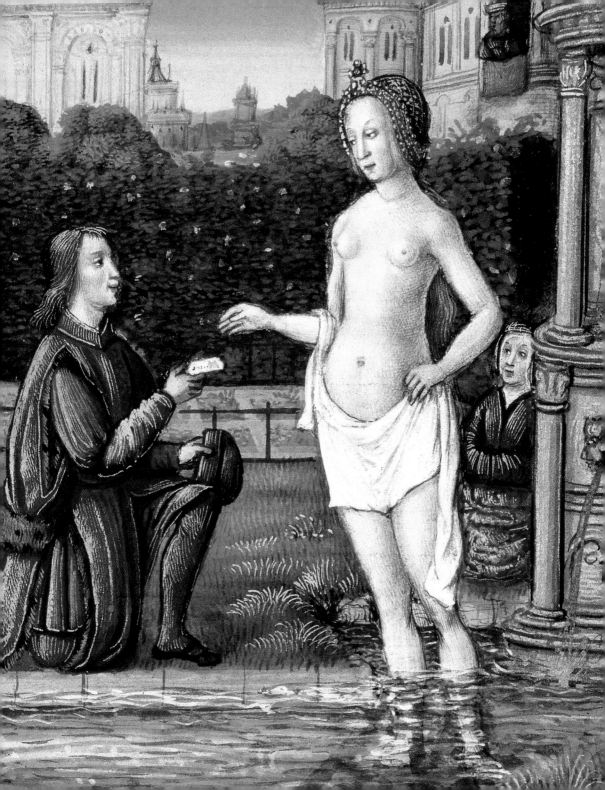

MY CONCUBINE

During those years I lived with a woman, although she was not joined to me in lawful marriage. I had come across her at a time when I was a victim of restless passion and unable to behave rationally, but she remained my only woman and I was faithful to her. In this relationship I learned from my own experience the difference between a marriage which is entered into for the sake of having children and an agreement based on lust in which the birth of a child is unwelcome – although if a child is born, its parents cannot help but love it. (4:2,2)

THE PLEASURE OF FRIENDSHIP

During those years when I first began to teach in the town where I was born, I had a friend who was very dear to me on account of our shared interests. We were the same age, both in the flower of our youth. As a boy he had grown up with me and we had gone to the same school and played together, although at that time he was not yet my friend. Even when he did become my friend it was not a true friendship, which is only possible when you, Lord, provide the glue, bonding friends together with the love that is poured into our hearts by the Holy Spirit who is granted to us. Yet it was a very sweet friendship, welded by the intensity of our shared interests. As a boy he held to the true faith but not firmly or deeply, and I had managed to turn him away from it, towards those superstitious and dangerous myths that caused my mother to shed tears for me. So as a young man in my company, his mind went astray, and my soul was lost without him. But you were right behind me as I fled from you, at once both God of vengeance and source of mercy, for you bring us back to yourself in ways we cannot understand. You took my friend from this life when our friendship was scarcely a year old, a relationship that was sweeter than anything else in my life at that time. (4:4,7)

MOURNING A FRIEND

When my friend died, grief darkened my heart and wherever I looked, all I could see was death. My home town was a torture to me and my family home a place of misery. All that I had shared with my friend became excruciating without him. My eyes looked for him everywhere but could not find him. I hated everything because he was absent; nowhere I went to could say to me, 'Look, here he is,' as it did when he was alive but not with me. I examined my feelings meticulously, asking my soul again and again why it was wretched and why it was causing me such distress, but it could give me no answer. Yet if I had said to my soul, 'Put your trust in God', it would have had good reason not to obey, because the precious friend I had lost was more adequate and more real to me than the shadowy being I was telling my soul to trust. Only tears were sweet to me; they had replaced my friend as my soul's delight. (4:4,9)

THE TORMENT OF GRIEF

Why do I mention all this? Now is not the time to analyze but to make my confession to you. I was in misery, as is every soul which is bound by a love of things that cannot last and tormented when it loses them. It is then the soul realizes the wretched state it was in even before its loss.

This was my situation at that time. I wept bitterly and found consolation in my bitterness. I was in such misery, and yet I was more attached to my life of unhappiness than to my dead friend. Although I wanted things to change, I was less willing to lose my grief than I had been to lose my friend. I do not know whether I would have been willing to die for him in the way that Orestes and Pylades, if the story is true, were willing to die together for each other, because each preferred to die than live without the other. And yet a strange feeling had grown in me, and it was very different from theirs: I was sick and tired of living but I was too afraid to die. It was as if the more I had loved my friend, the more I hated and feared the force that had taken

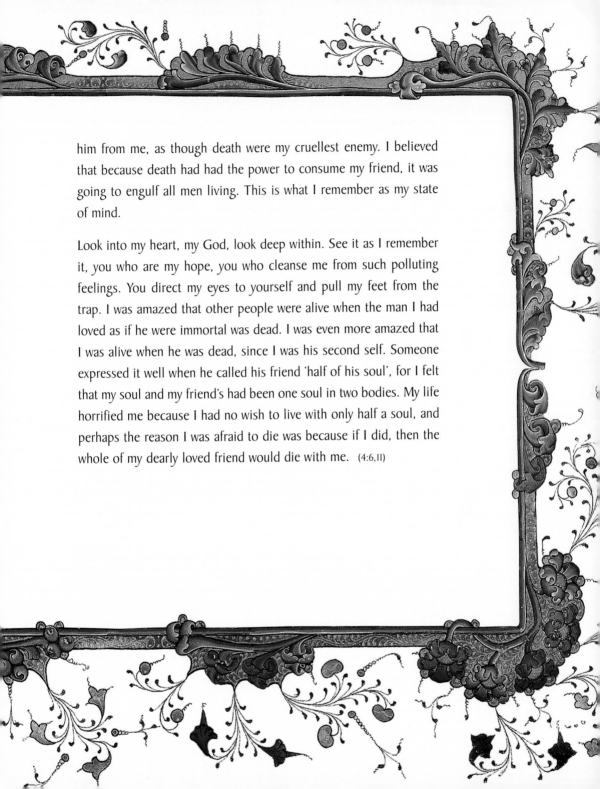

him from me, as though death were my cruellest enemy. I believed that because death had had the power to consume my friend, it was going to engulf all men living. This is what I remember as my state of mind.

Look into my heart, my God, look deep within. See it as I remember it, you who are my hope, you who cleanse me from such polluting feelings. You direct my eyes to yourself and pull my feet from the trap. I was amazed that other people were alive when the man I had loved as if he were immortal was dead. I was even more amazed that I was alive when he was dead, since I was his second self. Someone expressed it well when he called his friend 'half of his soul', for I felt that my soul and my friend's had been one soul in two bodies. My life horrified me because I had no wish to live with only half a soul, and perhaps the reason I was afraid to die was because if I did, then the whole of my dearly loved friend would die with me. (4:6,11)

TIME'S HEALING POWER

Time does not stand still, and its passing has a remarkable effect on our feelings and our souls. From one day to the next, time came and went, and the coming and going planted new hopes in me and fresh memories. Gradually it repaired me by means of the pleasures that I had enjoyed in the past, and my unhappiness yielded to them. My grief was replaced not by new sorrows but by the causes of new sorrows. How had that grief penetrated me so easily and so deeply? Was it not because I had poured out my soul onto the sand by loving someone who was mortal as if he were immortal? What restored and revived me most effectively, my God, was the solace provided by other friends, with whom I loved what I loved as a substitute for you.

(4:8,13)

A BEGGAR'S HAPPINESS

I desired status, wealth and marriage but you laughed at me. I suffered from the most bitter frustration of my ambitions but it was your kindness that let me find no sweetness in anything that was not you. Look into my heart, Lord, you who wanted me to recall this and confess to you. May my soul cling to you now, for you have pulled it away from the birdlime of death in which it was stuck fast. How unhappy was my soul! You probed my wound to the quick to make my soul abandon all ambition and turn to you – who are above all things and without whom all things would be nothing – so that, by turning to you, my wound should be healed.

How desolate I was! You managed to make me aware of my despair one day as I was preparing to deliver a speech in praise of the Emperor. I was to tell many lies that would be enjoyed by people who would know full well they were not the truth. My heart pounded with anxiety, my thoughts gnawed away at me and put me in a feverish sweat. As I walked along the street in Milan, I noticed a destitute beggar who, I think, was already drunk, because he was joking and laughing.

I exclaimed sadly and spoke to my companions about the suffering that results from our delusions. All our efforts such as those then causing me anxiety – as my ambitions forced me to drag along the burden of my unhappiness, which just made it the more oppressive – were directed at nothing more than the attainment of a state of carefree pleasure. But the beggar had got there first – and perhaps we never would attain it. For what he had gained with a few coins got by begging – namely, the pleasure of temporary happiness – I was striving to find in such distressingly twisted and roundabout ways.

Not that the beggar possessed true joy; but my method of seeking fulfilment through corrupt practices was far more false. Certainly, he was cheerful while I was anxious; he was carefree while I was filled with apprehension; and if anyone were to ask me whether I would prefer to be cheerful or afraid, I would answer, 'to be cheerful'. But if I were then asked whether I would prefer to be like the beggar or like myself, as I was at the time, I would choose to be myself, though consumed by anxieties and fears. Yet that would surely be a perverse and dishonest answer. For I ought not to prefer myself to him for being better educated, seeing that this had given me no happiness. Instead, my education only made me keen to please people – and with a view not to instructing them but only to giving them pleasure. And so you broke my bones with the rod of your discipline. (6:6,9)

DESIRE AND MARRIAGE

It was Alypius who held me back from marriage. His reasoning was that if I were to marry there would be no way we would be able to live together without distractions and with the leisure to devote ourselves to philosophy, as we had long planned to do. By this time he himself had attained complete self-control in sexual matters, which I found remarkable. He had experienced sexual intercourse in early adolescence but had not continued with it – in fact, he had regretted and condemned it, and had thereafter lived a life of complete abstinence. I refused to be persuaded, citing examples of people who, although married, had also managed to pursue philosophy, please God and maintain loyal and loving friendships. Such people were far superior to me in nobility of soul for I was fettered by the fatal attraction of physical desire and I dragged this chain of mine along with me, afraid to be free of it. I rejected Alypius' persuasive words as if they were a hand loosening that chain, for he touched a sore point with me. Furthermore, when I gave my answers to Alypius, the serpent used my tongue to lay tempting snares in his path, aimed at trapping his virtuous and unfettered feet.

Alypius found it incredible that I, whom he regarded so highly, should be caught in the birdlime of sexual pleasure. Whenever we discussed the matter, I would claim that it was beyond me to lead a life of celibacy. I defended myself when I saw his amazement, arguing that there was a world of difference between his hasty, furtive experience – which he could now barely even remember and was therefore all too easy to condemn – and my enjoyment of a long-term relationship. If it were dignified with the name of marriage, I pointed out, he would not be surprised that I found it hard to give up. And so it was that he himself began to desire marriage, overcome not by lust but by curiosity. He said he wanted to know what it was without which my life would have seemed to me not life but torture, though he found such a life perfectly acceptable. While his mind was free from these bonds, he was astonished by my enslavement, but his astonishment passed into a desire to experience the same thing. If he had, he would perhaps have fallen into that very state of slavery that so surprised him, since he wanted to make a pact with death, and anyone who courts danger is bound to become its victim.

Neither of us thought very seriously about the benefits to be had from steering a course through married life and in bringing up children. To a large extent I was a prisoner of habit, tormented by my attempts to satisfy an insatiable sexual desire, while it was curiosity that drew Alypius towards captivity. This was how things were until you, God most high, took pity on us. You did not abandon the dust from which we are formed; and you came to our aid in ways both wonderful and incomprehensible. (6:12,21–6:12,22)

MY SEARCH FOR YOU

As I pursued my desperate search in silence, the unspoken despondency I felt in my heart pleaded loudly for your mercy. You knew what it was I suffered, but no man did. How little of it my tongue was able to put into words for the ears of my closest friends! I had neither sufficient time nor the eloquence to tell them of the storm raging in my soul. Yet as I roared and groaned deep in my heart, you heard it all clearly; you knew what I desired, and the light of my eyes was not with me but within me, even as I looked outwards. It did not shine in the world around me, yet my attention rested on things that were contained in that space, and I found no place there to rest, nor did these outward things welcome me so that I could say, 'This is as it should be; this is what I wanted'; nor did they allow me to return to a place where all would be like this. I was on a higher plane than these external objects but I was lower than you. You are my true joy if I recognize that I am subject to you, and that you made subject to me all you created to be lower than me. This would have ensured the proper balance, the intermediate position that would lead to salvation, allowing me to remain in your image and, in serving you, to be master of my body. (7:7,II)

THE LIGHT OF GOD

The books of Platonic philosophy I read encouraged me to return to myself and, with you as my guide, I entered inside the innermost part of my soul, able to do so because you were helping me. I entered and with the eye of my soul – such as it was – glimpsed the immutable light that shines above that eye, higher than my mind. It was no ordinary light: not the light that is known by every living creature, nor even a greater version of it, which would have shone far more brightly and filled everywhere around it with its intensity. It was not like that, but completely different from all these kinds of light. It did not shine above my mind in the way that oil floats on top of water or the sky hangs above the earth; it was above me because it had created me and I was below it because I was created by it. All who know the truth know this light, and all who know this light know eternity. Love knows this light. Eternal truth and true love and beloved eternity, you are my God; to you I sigh day and night. When I first knew you, you raised me up so that I could see that what I saw existed and understand that I who saw it did not yet exist. Your radiance blinded me and I trembled with love and awe. I realized that I was far from you, in a place where the differences between us were distinct; and I seemed to hear your voice far above me saying, 'I am the food of the fully grown; grow and you will feed on me. You will not change me into yourself like the food your body eats, but you will be transformed into me.' (7:10,16)

THE NATURE OF GOODNESS

I t became clear to me that things which are subject to corruption must be good, for if they were perfect, or not good at all, they could not be corrupted. If they were perfect it follows that they would be incorruptible; if they were not good at all there would be nothing in them that was capable of being corrupted. Corruption is an agent of harm but if it is not taking away from what is good, it is causing no harm. Therefore either corruption causes no harm – and that is impossible – or everything that is corrupted is deprived of goodness – which is definitely the case. If things are deprived of all goodness they cease to exist; if they exist and are immune from corruption, they must be perfect because they are incorruptible. What is more absurd than saying that something is better when it is deprived of all its goodness? If things are deprived of all goodness they will be nothing at all; consequently, as long as they exist they must be good.

So whatever exists is good, and the evil whose origin I was trying to locate is not a substance, for if it were a substance it would be good: it would either be an incorruptible substance – a good of a high order indeed – or a corruptible substance which unless it were good could not be corrupted. It became clear to me: I saw that all the things you created are good and that there is no substance that you did not create. But as you did not make everything equal, all things are good in themselves, and all things together are very good because our God made all things very good.

I turned my attention to other things and saw that they owe their existence to you. In you all things are finite, not in the sense that they are bounded by space, but in the sense that you hold all things in your truth and all things are true in so far as they exist. Falsehood only applies when something that is thought to exist does not. I saw, too, that each thing is not only suited to its place but also to its time, and that you alone are eternal. You did not begin your work after innumerable periods of time because all periods of time, both past and future, come into being and pass away only if you, who abides forever, make them do so. (7:12,18 and 7:15,21)

THE NON-EXISTENCE OF EVIL

For you evil does not exist, and not only for you but for the whole of your creation, because there is nothing outside it that could break in and threaten the order you have imposed on it. In parts of your creation, some things are regarded as evil because they are in conflict with other elements, yet they are in harmony with others and as such they can be regarded as good, and in themselves they are good. And all these things that war against each other are at one with the lesser part of creation which we call earth. There is no incongruity, for example, between the earth and the sky with its clouds and wind.

Far be it from me to wish that these things did not exist: if they were all I could see, it is true that I might wish for better, but even taken on their own, I should still praise you for them. For all things born of the earth show us that you deserve praise: sea monsters and the sea depths, fire and hail, snow and frost, the breath of the storm which does as you ask, mountains and all hills, fruit trees and all cedars, wild animals and all cattle, reptiles and winged birds; kings of the earth and all peoples, princes and all rulers of the earth, young men and women, old and young together: let them praise you. Let them also praise you from the heavens, let them exalt you, our God,

your angels on high, all your powers, sun and moon, all the stars and light, the heaven of heavens and the waters above the heavens: let them praise your name.

I no longer wished for things to be better, because I regarded everything as part of a whole. Admittedly, I still used to judge those things on a higher level as better than those on a lower level but because I now had a healthier view of things, I held the entirety to be better than these superior things taken on their own. (7:13,19)

THAT WHICH IS

I was amazed to discover that I already loved you, rather than some illusion of you. And yet I was unable to enjoy my God for any length of time: I was swept towards you by your beauty but almost immediately torn away from you by my own weight, falling back into the material world with a groan. This weight was my sexual habit. But I did not forget you; I had no doubt that you were the one to whom I should cling, even though I was not yet able to because the mortal body weighs down the soul, and our earthly habitation oppresses the active mind. Moreover, I was utterly certain that since the beginning of the world your invisible nature – your eternal power and divinity – have been seen and understood through your creation.

I wondered why I admired physical bodies, whether celestial or earthbound, and how it was I could make value judgements such as, 'This ought to be like this; that should not be like that.' When I tried to understand why I did this, I found the fixed and true eternity of your truth above my changeable mind. And so, step by step, I first ascended from the body to the soul that perceives through the body, and from there to the inner energy of the soul to which the body's senses communicate external sensations – this being as much as animals can achieve. Next I ascended to the power of reason, which has the ability to judge what is delivered to it by means of the senses. This power, which I found also fickle in me, raised itself up to its own intelligence, diverting my thoughts away from their habitual channels and withdrawing itself from the jumble of contradictory images so as to discover by what light it was illuminated. At this level, reason asserted without doubt that the immutable is better than the changeable, and that – following this logic – it must therefore know the immutable, because otherwise it would have no way of knowing that it was preferable to the changeable.

And so it was that, in a flash of perception, I reached that which is. I saw and understood your invisible nature through those things which are created. Yet I could not keep my eyes fixed and my weakness pushed me back and returned me to my ordinary state. I retained only the memory of something I loved and desired, as if it were a delicious food which I could smell but was not yet allowed to eat. (7:17,23)

THE ATTRACTIONS OF SIN

My thoughts as I meditated on you were like those of someone who is trying to wake but is overwhelmed by tiredness and sinks back into a deep sleep. No one wants to sleep all the time, and we all know that it is better to be awake, but we often put off waking while our limbs are heavy with sleep: although it is time to get up we are happy to snatch a bit more sleep even though we know it is wrong. In the same way, I was convinced that it was better for me to surrender to your love than yield to my self-indulgence and yet, while I wanted to follow the former course and believed it to be right, the latter was more attractive and got the better of me. I had no answer for you when you said, 'Get up, sleepy one, rise up from the dead and Christ will give you light.' You gave me all kinds of proof that what you said was true and I was sure of the truth, but I could only reply in a sluggish and drowsy way, 'Soon'— 'In a moment'— 'Just a little longer'—. But my 'Soon, soon' was not soon, and my 'Just a little longer' went on for a long time. There was no point in my approving your law with regard to my inmost self when another law in my body was at war with my mind, binding me to the law of sin. For the law of sin is the force of habit by which the mind is hauled off and held against its will – as it deserves to be, since it is by its own choice that it slips into this habit. Wretched creature that I was, who was to set me free from this doomed body other than your grace through Jesus Christ our Lord? (8:5,12)

SAINT ANTONY

One day Alypius and I received a visit at home from a man named Ponticianus, a fellow countryman of ours (being from Africa), who held high office at the imperial court. He had some request or other and we sat down to discuss it – only there happened to be a book lying on the gaming table in front of us and he picked it up, opened it and found that it contained the letters of Saint Paul the Apostle. He was no doubt surprised because he had thought it would be a book connected with the profession which was grinding me down at the time. He smiled and looked at me as if to say, 'Well done!', apparently amazed to have suddenly discovered that I was reading this particular book.

When I told Ponticianus that I had studied those writings with the utmost attention, he mentioned the Egyptian monk Antony, who was very well known among your servants although Alypius and I had never heard of him until that moment. When he discovered this, he was shocked by our ignorance and told the story in greater detail because he wanted us to know something of this great man. We were astonished to hear about the well-attested miracles that had been performed so recently – almost in our own day – by this person who followed the orthodox doctrine of the Catholic Church. In fact, we were all somewhat taken aback: Alypius and I because of the greatness of the miracles, and Ponticianus because we had never heard of Antony and these miracles before. (8:6,14)

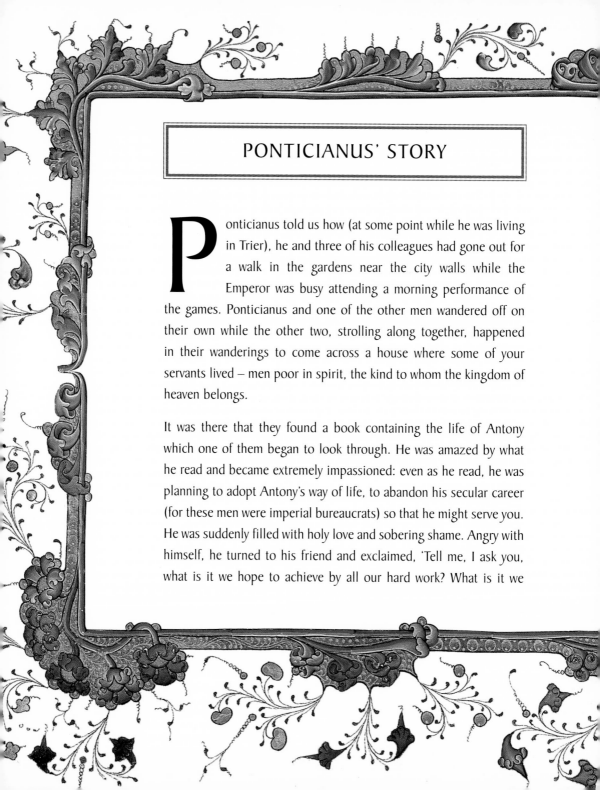

PONTICIANUS' STORY

onticianus told us how (at some point while he was living in Trier), he and three of his colleagues had gone out for a walk in the gardens near the city walls while the Emperor was busy attending a morning performance of the games. Ponticianus and one of the other men wandered off on their own while the other two, strolling along together, happened in their wanderings to come across a house where some of your servants lived – men poor in spirit, the kind to whom the kingdom of heaven belongs.

It was there that they found a book containing the life of Antony which one of them began to look through. He was amazed by what he read and became extremely impassioned: even as he read, he was planning to adopt Antony's way of life, to abandon his secular career (for these men were imperial bureaucrats) so that he might serve you. He was suddenly filled with holy love and sobering shame. Angry with himself, he turned to his friend and exclaimed, 'Tell me, I ask you, what is it we hope to achieve by all our hard work? What is it we

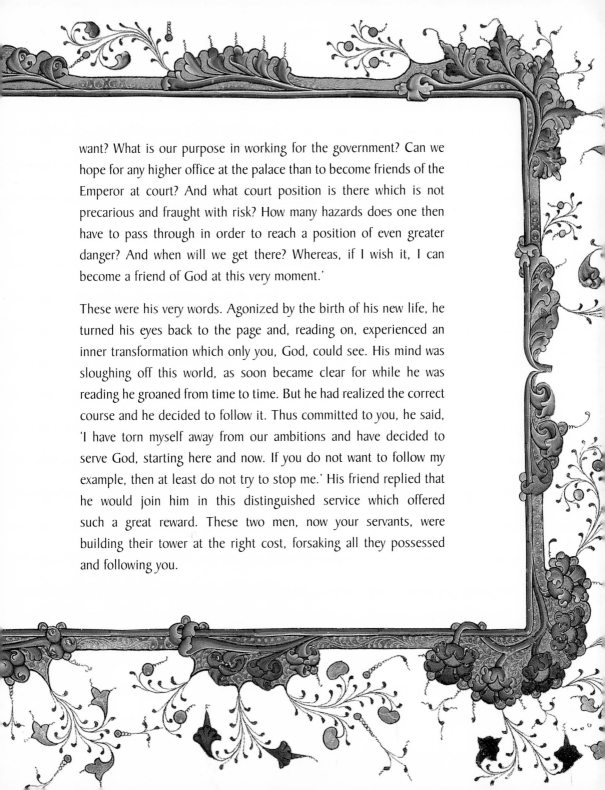

want? What is our purpose in working for the government? Can we hope for any higher office at the palace than to become friends of the Emperor at court? And what court position is there which is not precarious and fraught with risk? How many hazards does one then have to pass through in order to reach a position of even greater danger? And when will we get there? Whereas, if I wish it, I can become a friend of God at this very moment.'

These were his very words. Agonized by the birth of his new life, he turned his eyes back to the page and, reading on, experienced an inner transformation which only you, God, could see. His mind was sloughing off this world, as soon became clear for while he was reading he groaned from time to time. But he had realized the correct course and he decided to follow it. Thus committed to you, he said, 'I have torn myself away from our ambitions and have decided to serve God, starting here and now. If you do not want to follow my example, then at least do not try to stop me.' His friend replied that he would join him in this distinguished service which offered such a great reward. These two men, now your servants, were building their tower at the right cost, forsaking all they possessed and following you.

Meanwhile Ponticianus and his companion, who had been walking in another part of the gardens, came to find them at the house. The daylight was already beginning to fade so they suggested that it was time to return home. But their colleagues told them of their decision and their plans, explaining what had brought about this change of course and how it had developed into a firm resolve. They begged their friends, even if they refused to join them, not to try and stop them. Ponticianus and his friend were not persuaded, but nonetheless they shed some tears for themselves and offered their colleagues heartfelt congratulations, asking to be remembered in their prayers. Then they returned to the palace, their hearts still bound to earth, while the other two remained in the house with their hearts fixed on heaven. Both of these men were engaged to be married but when their fiancées heard what had happened they, too, decided to dedicate their chastity to you. (8:6,15)

YOU MADE ME FACE MYSELF

While Ponticianus continued with his story, you turned me round to face myself, Lord. You took me from behind my back, where I had positioned myself because I refused to look at myself, and you placed me before my face so that I could see how disgusting I was, how grotesque and covered in blotches and sores. I was shocked by what I saw but there was no escape. Even when I tried to avert my gaze, I was still forced to go on listening to Ponticianus' story and by this means you made me confront myself again, placing me once more before my eyes so that I should discover my wickedness and grow to hate it. I had been aware of it, only pretended it did not exist; I had suppressed the knowledge and tried to forget it. But at that moment, as my heart warmed to those young men whose longing for spiritual health had led them to dedicate themselves wholly to you so that you might heal them, I began to hate myself in comparison.

Many years – about twelve – had passed since my nineteenth year when I had read Cicero's *Hortensius* and been stimulated by this work to search for wisdom. But although I had developed a contempt for worldly success, I had put off finding the time to seek out wisdom.

Yet the search for wisdom, let alone its discovery, should be valued more highly than the discovery of all the world's treasures and kingdoms, more highly than all those physical pleasures I could command at will. I was an unhappy young man, as despairing as I had been as an adolescent when I had prayed to you for chastity with the words, 'Grant me chastity and the will to abstain, but not yet.' I was afraid then that you would hear my prayer too quickly and cure me of the disease of lust which I preferred to appease rather than to suppress.

Now the time had come for me to be stripped naked before myself, and my conscience rebuked me, asking, 'What has happened to your tongue? I thought you said you could not cast off the burden of your empty life while you still had doubts about the truth? Yet now you have no more doubts, and still this burden oppresses you, while these people who have not exhausted themselves with ten years or more of endless searching and thinking have cast off their burdens and taken on wings.' (8:7,16–8:7,18)

LADY CONTINENCE

In the midst of the furious struggle I was having with my soul in the inner room of my spiritual house that is my heart, I turned on Alypius, who could see from my face how distressed I was, and cried out, 'What is happening to us? What is this story you have heard? Uneducated people are rising up and taking heaven by storm while we with all our soulless learning are wallowing in flesh and blood! Is it because they are ahead that we are ashamed to follow? Are we not ashamed that we do not even attempt to follow them?' This was the gist of what I said. In my passion I did not notice that Alypius was looking at me in stunned silence – for I was not speaking in my normal manner. In fact, my brow, my cheeks, eyes, colour and the tone of my voice told him more about my state of mind than did my actual words.

There happened to be a garden behind the house where we were lodging. We had the use of this as well as of the entire house because our landlord was not living there. The turmoil I was experiencing compelled me to rush out into the garden, where the violent struggle I was engaged in could take its course without interruption. You knew what the outcome would be but I did not. My madness was a step towards sanity: by dying, I was becoming alive. I was aware of how ill I was but unaware of how much better I was soon to be.

So I hurried out into the garden with Alypius hard on my heels. His presence did not disturb my solitude. How could he abandon me in such a state? We sat down as far as possible from the house. I was deeply disturbed, angry and upset that I was not entering a union with you according to your will, my God, although every bone in my body was crying out for me to do so, praising it to the skies. But this is not the sort of journey one makes by ship or chariot or on foot – I did not even need to go as far as the distance between the house and the place where we were sitting. For not only going but even reaching this place required no more than the will to go, providing the will was resolute and sincere and more than a half-hearted wish, twisting and turning this way and that, struggling as one part of it manages to lift itself while another part collapses.

My old friends, frivolous desires and empty ambitions, were holding me back. Tugging at the garment of my flesh, they whispered, 'Are you sending us away?' and 'From this moment on you will never be allowed to do this or that.' What were they implying by what I have termed 'this or that'? May your mercy, my God, keep such things away from the soul of your servant! What sordid and shameful things they were suggesting! But their voices seemed far away and I was only half listening: they were not confronting me openly but as it were muttering behind my back, furtively grabbing me as I moved away from them, in an effort to make me turn round and look at them. They

hampered my attempts to shake them off, to break free and leap across to the place to which I felt myself summoned, and at the same time the potent force of habit continued to ask me, 'Do you really think you can manage without these things?'

However, it was speaking in a more half-hearted way now and, from the place I was facing but which I was afraid to cross over to, the chaste and dignified Lady Continence appeared before me. She stood there serene and cheerful, with no hint of flirtatiousness, inviting me to come to her without hesitation and stretching out loving hands to receive me in her embrace. (8:8,19 and 8:11,26–8:11,27)

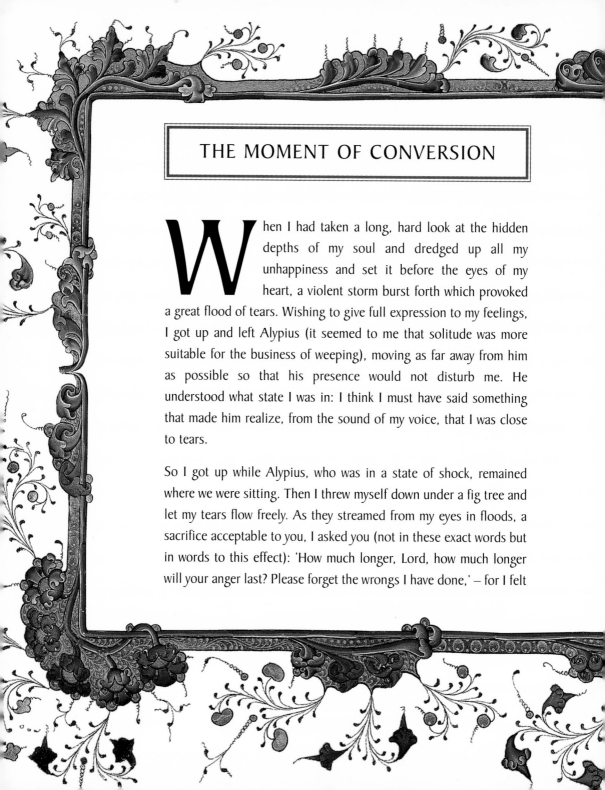

THE MOMENT OF CONVERSION

When I had taken a long, hard look at the hidden depths of my soul and dredged up all my unhappiness and set it before the eyes of my heart, a violent storm burst forth which provoked a great flood of tears. Wishing to give full expression to my feelings, I got up and left Alypius (it seemed to me that solitude was more suitable for the business of weeping), moving as far away from him as possible so that his presence would not disturb me. He understood what state I was in: I think I must have said something that made him realize, from the sound of my voice, that I was close to tears.

So I got up while Alypius, who was in a state of shock, remained where we were sitting. Then I threw myself down under a fig tree and let my tears flow freely. As they streamed from my eyes in floods, a sacrifice acceptable to you, I asked you (not in these exact words but in words to this effect): 'How much longer, Lord, how much longer will your anger last? Please forget the wrongs I have done,' – for I felt that these still had a grip on me – and I cried out in anguish, 'How long will I keep saying, "tomorrow, tomorrow"? Why not now? Why not put an end to my sinful behaviour this very moment?'

While I was saying these things and weeping with bitter remorse, I suddenly heard a voice from the house next door – I am not sure whether it was a boy or a girl – chanting and repeating over and over again, 'Pick it up and read, pick it up and read.' My expression changed immediately and, concentrating as hard as I could, I tried to remember if this was a popular song used in some children's game, but I could not recall ever having heard it. I checked the flood of my tears and stood up. The only interpretation I could give this was that a divine command was telling me to open the book and read the first chapter I came across. I had heard that Antony had been guided by a Gospel reading he happened to have heard, as if the text was being addressed specifically to him when it said, 'Go, sell all you have, give to the poor and you will have treasure in heaven, and come and follow me.' Those words had been like an oracle and brought about his immediate conversion to you. So I returned in excitement to where Alypius was sitting, for that was where I had left the book of Saint Paul's letters when I got up to leave. I seized the book, opened it and read in silence the first verses on which my eyes chanced to fall: 'Not in partying and drunkenness, not in lust and immoral acts, not in quarrels and jealousy, but put on the Lord Jesus Christ and do not be concerned to gratify the desires of the flesh.'

I did not read any further: there was no need. As soon as I finished reading this verse, my heart was flooded with a light of certainty that put to flight all the darkness of my doubt. Keeping the place with my finger or some other marker, I closed the book and, with a calm expression, told Alypius what had happened. He revealed to me what was going on in his mind – which I did not know – in the following way: he asked to see what I had read. When I showed him the text, he noticed the passage that followed on from it. I was not familiar with the way the text went on: 'Receive the person who is weak in faith.' Alypius took these words to apply to himself and showed them to me. The admonition gave him confidence and, without hesitation, he joined me in taking the decisive step of committing ourselves to that excellent way of life, perfectly suited to his moral state which had long been superior to mine. (8:12,28–8:12,30)

WHO AM I?

Who am I and what am I? What was not wicked in my deeds – or, if not in my deeds, then in my words, or if not in my words, then in my intentions? But you, Lord, are good and compassionate. You were able to look deep within me and see that I was spiritually dead; you drained the deep well of corruption at the bottom of my heart. All I had to do was reject what I wanted and accept what you wanted. Yet where was my free will during those long years? From what remote depths was it brought forth so that, all at once, I could bend my neck to your comfortable yoke and my shoulders to your light burden, Christ Jesus, my helper and redeemer? Suddenly I found it delightful to be without those trivial pleasures that I had feared to lose and was now glad to reject. You threw them out of me, you who are the true and perfect pleasure, and replaced them with yourself; sweeter than every desire, though not to flesh and blood, brighter than any light but deeper within my heart than its most secret recess, higher than any honour but not to those who think highly of themselves. My mind was at last free from the gnawing cares of ambition, of the hunger for gain; free to stop wallowing in self-indulgence and picking at the scab of lust. I was now talking freely to you, Lord God, my light, my wealth and my salvation. (9:I,I)

A VISION AT OSTIA

The day was at hand when my mother was to depart this life (you knew the day but we did not). It happened – I believe providentially, though your ways are hidden from us – that she and I were standing leaning out of a window that looked out onto the garden of our lodgings at Ostia on the Tiber. Alone in that quiet spot, we were resting after a long and exhausting journey and preparing ourselves for the voyage ahead. We talked very pleasantly together, putting the past behind us and looking forward to the future. We wondered, in the presence of reality that is you, what the everlasting life of the saints might be like, a life which no eye has seen nor ear heard nor human heart conceived. We felt a spiritual thirst to drink from your heavenly spring, the fountain of life that is with you, for we hoped that just a few drops might give us an inkling of your wondrous truth.

Our conversation led us to conclude that no bodily pleasure, however delightful in the light of this material world, can be compared with the joy of that eternal life. Our fervent longing for that eternal being raised us up towards you and, step by step, we passed beyond all physical things, through heaven itself from where the sun and moon and stars shine down upon the earth. We ascended still further by means of contemplation and discussion and wonder at your works; we entered our minds and transcended them so as to reach the region of inexhaustible plenty where you feed Israel for ever with the food of truth. There life is that wisdom by which all things are made, those that have been and those that will be. This wisdom was not created but is now as it was and will be for ever, or rather, since it has no past or future, there is only being, for it is eternal and one cannot say of eternity that it was or will be. As we talked, we focused on it with a deep longing, striving to reach it until – in a moment of total concentration – we were able at last to touch it. We sighed as we then left behind the first fruits of the spirit and returned to the noise of our human speech, in which each word has a beginning and an end. Nothing can compare with your Word, our Lord, which remains in you for ever: it never grows old and it breathes new life into all there is.

And so we said: If this state were to continue and all other visions of an inferior kind could be lost while this one alone took hold of the soul gazing upon it, absorbing it and enveloping it in spiritual joy, then this is what eternal life would be like, just like that moment of understanding for which we longed. Is this not what is meant by Christ's words in the parable, 'Enter into the joy of your Lord'? When shall this happen? Surely it will be when all of us rise again although we will not all be changed. (9:10,23–9:10,25)

THE VALUE OF CONFESSION

L ord, the whole of man's conscience lies revealed to your eyes: what could stay hidden within me even if I refused to confess it to you? I could hide from myself but not from you. Yet now my groans prove my displeasure with myself. You shine brightly and give happiness and are an object of love and longing, while I am ashamed of myself and reject myself. I choose you and I cannot please myself or you unless you allow me to do so. Whatever I am, you see me clearly. I have already spoken of the good I derive from confessing to you: I do not do this with physical words and sounds but with words from my soul; my thoughts shout out to you so that you may hear them. For when I am bad, confessing to you is merely disapproval of myself, but when I am good, confessing to you is simply admitting that I am not good of my own accord, for it is you, Lord, who confers blessings on the just, but only after you have first made them just when they were wicked.

Therefore, my God, my confession to you is both silent and not silent: silent in that no sound is made, but not silent in that my feelings cry out loud. If anything I say to people is true, it is only after you have first heard it from me, and if you hear anything true from me, it is only what you have told me before.

Why then should I be concerned for men to hear my confessions, as if it were they who were going to heal all my sicknesses? Men are keen to learn about the lives of other people but lazy when it comes to correcting their own. Why do people demand to hear from me what I am when they refuse to hear from you what they are? And when they hear me talking about myself, how do they know whether I am telling the truth, since no one knows what is going on in a person except the spirit of each individual which is within them? Yet if you were to tell them about themselves, they could not say, 'The Lord is lying', for to hear you speaking about oneself is to know oneself.

(10:2,2–10:3,3)

er augustine, preces nras

susap̃r. ce peras ꝯ dicon.

MY LOVE FOR YOU, LORD

I do not doubt my love for you, Lord: I know for certain that I love you. Your words pierced my heart and I fell in love with you. And, furthermore, heaven and earth and all that is around me cries out that I should love you, never ceasing to proclaim to all men that there is no excuse not to love you. But at a deeper level you will have mercy on whom you will have mercy and you will have compassion on whom you will have compassion: otherwise heaven and earth would be pouring out your praises on deaf ears.

But what do I love when I love you? Not a material attraction or beauty, which lasts but a moment; nor the brightness of light that is all around us, so welcome to our eyes; nor the sweet melodies of every kind of song; nor the lovely fragrance of flowers, perfumes and spices; nor manna and honey; nor the limbs of the body, so delightful to embrace. It is not these things that I love when I love my God. And yet, when I love him, I do love a kind of light and voice and fragrance and food and embrace – but the light and voice and fragrance and food and embrace of my inner self. There, my soul is illuminated with light unbounded by space; it listens to sounds that time cannot snatch away; there is fragrance that the breezes do not dispel; taste that does not diminish with eating; and my soul clings in an embrace from which it cannot be torn away by satisfied desire. All this is what I love when I love my God. (10:6,8)

WHAT IS MEMORY?

What am I then, my God? What is my nature? Life is full of variety and impossible to measure. Consider the broad expanses of my memory, its innumerable caverns and lairs. Each one is filled with countless different things, placed there either by means of images, as in the case of all physical objects, or by their actual presence, as in the case of skills, or through some notion or impression, as in the case of the emotions (for even when the mind is not experiencing these, they are still retained in the memory, although whatever is in the memory is in the mind). I run through all these things, darting this way and that and delving into them as deeply as possible but I never come to the end. So great is the power of memory, so vibrant is the force of the life of man even though it is mortal.

What then should I do, my God, you who are my true life? I will pass through this faculty of mine that is called memory; I will transcend it to reach you, sweet light. What is it you are saying to me? Look how

I am rising upwards through my mind towards you who are always above me. I am passing even beyond that power of mind that is called memory, for I wish to reach you by the only way it is possible, to cling to you in the only way I can. Birds and beasts also possess memory; otherwise they would not be able to find their way back to their nests and lairs or do all the many other things they are in the habit of – in fact, without memory, they would not have any habits. So I will transcend memory, too, in order to reach him who has set me apart from the four-footed creatures and made me wiser than the birds in the sky. I will transcend memory, too, so as to find you, my true good, my sweetness in whom I can trust. But where am I to find you? If I find you beyond my memory, then I have no memory of you. And if I have no memory of you, how can I find you? (10:17,26)

THE TRULY HAPPY LIFE

The truly happy life consists of looking to you for happiness, seeking it from you and through you. This is the only path to true joy. Those who think happiness is to be found in some other way are pursuing a different, false version of it, but in their minds they still retain some image of the true joy.

It is not clear, then, that everyone wants to be happy: there are some who refuse to look to you for their happiness although it is the only path to a truly happy life, and so it would seem that such people do not really want happiness. Or perhaps everyone does want happiness, but because the flesh lusts against the spirit and the spirit against the flesh and prevents people from doing what they would like, they relapse into whatever they can easily manage and are content with that. Their desire for what they cannot do is not strong enough to allow them to achieve it. If I ask someone whether they prefer to find happiness in truth or in falsehood, they do not hesitate to say that they prefer the truth, just as they would not hesitate to say that they want to be happy.

The happy life is joy based on truth, for this is the joy that comes from you, God, who are the truth; you, my God, are my illumination and the salvation of my face. Everyone yearns for this happy life; everyone desires this life which is the only one that brings happiness;

everyone desires the joy based on truth. I have come across many people who wished to deceive, but none who wished to be deceived. So how did they know about this happy life except in the same way that they knew about the truth? They love the truth because they do not want to be deceived, and when they love the happy life – which is the same as joy based on truth – they must also love the truth. It would be impossible for them to love the truth unless they had some notion of it in their memory. Why then do they not look for happiness in this way? Why are they not happy? Perhaps it is because they are engrossed in things that make them wretched and only have a dim memory of that which would give them joy. (10:22,32–10:23,33)

THE TEMPTATION TO POSSESS

Mankind has developed countless skills and methods for manufacturing clothes, shoes, utensils and so forth, and for creating pictures and all the various images of their imagination. In doing so they go far beyond their own modest needs or any devout purpose. Rather, they are motivated by a desire to seduce the eyes. Turning to external things, they pursue what they create; within themselves they neglect the one who created them and destroy what they were made to be. But for this reason, I will offer a hymn to you, my God and my glory, and make a sacrifice of praise to you who have made a sacrifice for me. For these beautiful things produced by the human soul and realized by skilled workmanship come from that beauty which is above our souls and for which my own soul longs day and night. Those artists who make beautiful objects, and those who desire to possess them, owe their ability to appreciate such things to this higher beauty, but this beauty is not responsible for their way of using them. It is there but they do not see it and so they move further away from it, not realizing that they should preserve their strength for you rather than wasting it on delights that make them weary. (10:34,53)

THE TEMPTATION OF KNOWLEDGE

There is another form of temptation far more dangerous than materialism. In addition to our physical desires, which are concerned with delighting all our senses and passions (and which destroy those people who are enslaved to them because they place themselves so far from you), there exists in the soul a certain desire to use these bodily senses not in the service of physical self-indulgence but as tools for gathering curious and useless facts. Attempts are made to render this cupidity more acceptable by referring to it as learning and knowledge. Since it is based on an appetite for knowing and the sense principally drawn on to acquire knowledge is sight, the Scriptures call it 'the lust of the eyes'.

When the senses demand pleasure, they seek gratification in beautiful things – in whatever sounds good, smells fragrant, tastes delicious or feels soft to the touch. But curiosity looks for satisfaction in the opposite of these things for it is driven by a lust to try things out, not because it wants to experience any discomfort, but because it has a passion for experimentation and discovery. What pleasure is to be derived from seeing a mangled corpse, an event which evokes horror? Yet when they see one lying somewhere, people crowd round in order to experience shock and sorrow. They even dread seeing this in their dreams, as if someone had forced them to look at it while they were awake or as if they had been misled into looking at it by a rumour that it was something beautiful.

The same is true of the other senses, though it would take too long to explore them all in this way. It is on account of this unhealthy craving that all sorts of shocking shows are put on; and it is for this reason that people strive to uncover nature's secrets although such things are beyond our understanding. There is no benefit to be gained from knowing these things: such people merely desire knowledge for its own sake. (10:35,54–10:35,55)

THE TEMPTATION TO SEEK APPROVAL

Certainly, the third kind of temptation has not ceased to affect me, and it will no doubt continue to exert an influence throughout my life. The temptation is to wish to be feared and loved by people simply for the pleasure this brings, though it is not a genuine happiness. It is a wretched life, a life of repulsive self-centredness. This especially is the cause of my inability to love and fear you in purity. For if we hold certain positions in society it is necessary for us to be both loved and feared by people, and the enemy of our true happiness keeps on attacking us, laying traps by repeating the words, 'Well done! Well done!' on every side. His aim is to catch us off guard while we are seeking approval of this kind and to force us to separate our happiness from your truth and base it instead on human deceitfulness. Our enemy wants us to be loved and feared not for your sake but instead of you. But this is wrong: we must be loved for your sake and it is your word in us that must be feared. Those who wish to be praised by others in the face of your rebukes will receive no human defence when you come to judge them, nor will they escape if you condemn them. (10:36,59)

TOWARDS TRUTH

Was there ever a time, Truth, when you did not walk beside me, teaching me what to avoid and what to look for whenever I reported what I could see in this earthly world and asked for your advice? I ranged over the external world as far as my mind allowed and studied the life of my own body and senses. Then I entered the recesses of my memory, vast areas of incredible variety, wondrously replete with countless riches. When I looked closely I was filled with awe. But it was impossible to see any of these things without you and I found that none of them was you. I realized that I had not discovered them, even though I had passed through them all and attempted to make distinctions and evaluate them according to their particular characteristics.

Some things I perceived by questioning the reports of my senses. Others I felt were mixed up with myself. I tried to identify and enumerate the various ways I received these messages and then, among the extensive riches of my memory, I studied other things, drawing out some of them and burying others. But even while I was doing this, you and I (that is, the faculty by which I did this) were not one and the same, for you are the eternal light by which I sought advice about all these things to discover whether they existed, what they were and what value I should attach to them: I listened to you teaching me and giving instructions. I often do this; it pleases me and, whenever the demands of my active life allow me to relax, I take refuge in this pleasure.

But in all these investigations I carry out with the help of your advice, the only safe place I can find for my soul is in you. Here, in my fragmented state, I am able to collect myself; no part of myself can depart from you. Sometimes you allow me to experience a feeling of strange and unfamiliar sweetness; if it were brought to perfection in me, it would be something that is not of this world. But then I fall back painfully into the world, weighed down by my human condition and sucked back into my ordinary state where, despite all my tears, I am held captive. So heavy is the burden of habit by which we are oppressed.   (10:40,65)

YOUR MERCY AND GOODNESS

I call upon you, my God, my mercy, who made me and did not forget me even when I forgot you. I call you into my soul which you are preparing to receive you through the longing you inspire in me. Do not abandon me now that I am calling upon you. Even before I called on you, you came to me and, with increasing insistence, put pressure on me, using many different voices to make me listen to you although I was far away in order to make me turn to you and call on you as you were calling on me. You wiped out all my bad deeds, Lord, so that you would not have to punish me as I deserved for the handiwork that made me unable to remain close to you. Instead you anticipated all my good deeds so that you could reward me for the work of your own hands which made me. For before I existed you were, and I had no being to which you could grant existence. Yet here I am as a result of your goodness, which goes before all that you made me to be and out of which you made me. You did not need me and I do not have sufficient goodness to help you, my Lord and my God. It is not as if I could serve you in such a way as to prevent you tiring in your work; your power would not be diminished if I did not look to you. I do not worship you in the way land is cultivated: you would not be unproductive if I failed to worship you, like a field that has not been ploughed. I serve you and worship you so that good may come to me from you; I owe my existence and my goodness to you. (13:1,1)

All illustrations are reproduced by kind permission of the British Library.

jacket: Harley MS 5370, f.165v
Book of Hours
Fifteenth century
St Augustine

back jacket; p.91: Add. MS 38897C
Italy, early fifteenth century
St Augustine blessing two groups of black canons who kneel at the steps of his throne.

pp.2–3; 94–5: (border, detail) Add. MS 18851, f.71
The Isabella Breviary
Flanders, Bruges; end of the fifteenth century; 230 x 160 mm
Christ tempted by the Devil in the Wilderness.

p.5: (detail) Add. MS 15254, f.13
Bible
Flanders; Liège; c.1430; 515 x 370 mm
The seven days of creation.

p.15: Royal MS 19 D. iii pt. 1, f.3
Bible Historiale
France; Paris, c.1411; 445 x 340 mm
Guyart des Moulins: God creating the world.

pp.16–17; 26–7; 38–9; 48–9; 58–9; 70–1; 82–3: (border, detail)
Harley MS 2897, f.380
Psalter
Fifteenth century
Border surrounding miniature of St Augustine.

p.19: Add. MS 18193, f.48v
Book of Hours
Spain; second half of the fifteenth century; 195 x 135 mm
The Holy Family in Joseph's carpenter's shop.

pp.20-21; 30–1; 42–3; 50–1; 64–5; 72–3; 88–9: (border, detail)
Harley MS 2936, ff.35v–36
Book of Hours
France; end of the fifteenth century; 155 x 105 mm
Border surrounding miniature of the shepherds adoring the Christ Child.

pp.22–3; 34–5; 46–7; 56–7; 66–7; 78–9: (border, detail)
Royal MS 8 G iii, f.2
Compendium super Bibliam
England; before 1422; 350 x 235 mm

Petrus de Aureolis: border surrounding miniature of a preaching Franciscan monk, the manuscript's author.

p.24: Add MS 18852, f.14v
Book of Hours
End of the fifteenth century
Eve offering the apple to Adam.

p.29: Harley MS 2969, f.91
The Hours of the Vasselin Family
Northwest France; early sixteenth century; 205 x 125 mm
Bathsheba accepting a letter from a messenger on behalf of King David, who leans out of the window.

p.32: Add. MS 18751, f.163
The Creméaux Hours
France, possibly Lyons; c.1440; 195 x 140 mm
Mourners attend a burial, while in the sky the Devil struggles with St Michael for the soul of the deceased.

p.37: Lansdowne MS 383, f.13
The Shaftesbury Psalter
England; c.1130–40; 220 x 130 mm
The three Marys at the tomb of Christ.

p.40: Add. MS 38125, f.58
Petrarch: *Poems*
Italy; end of the fifteenth century; 200 x 125 mm
Petrarch and Laura.

p.45: (detail) Add. MS 18850, f.15v
The Bedford Hours
France, Paris, c.1423; 260 x 180 mm
The construction of Noah's ark.

p.49: (detail) Add. MS 34294, f.38
The Sforza Hours
Italy, Milan; completed 1521; 131 x 93 mm
Giovan Pietro Birago: detail from decorative border.

p.53: Add. MS 18851, f.71
The Isabella Breviary
Flanders, Bruges; end of the fifteenth century; 230 x 160 mm
Christ tempted by the Devil in the Wilderness.

p.54: Harley MS 2897, f.380
Psalter

Fifteenth century
St Augustine

p.58: (detail) Add. MS 34294, f.272
The Sforza Hours
Italy, Milan; completed 1521; 131 x 93 mm
Giovan Pietro Birago: apostle praying, a detail from a miniature depicting the Virgin Mary's deathbed.

p.60: Add. MS 54782, f.265v
The Hastings Hours
Bruges or Ghent; before 1483; 165 x 120 mm
Christ washing the feet of his disciples.

p.63: Add. MS 18851, f.234
The Isabella Breviary
Flanders, Bruges; end of the fifteenth century; 230 x 160 mm
The descent of the Holy Spirit at Pentecost.

p.69: Add. MS 34294, f.198v
The Sforza Hours
Italy, Milan; completed 1521; 131 x 93 mm
Giovan Pietro Birago: St Ambrose.

p.74: Add. MS 34294, f.223
The Sforza Hours
Italy, Milan; completed 1521; 131 x 93 mm
Giovan Pietro Birago: The prophet Nathan berating the penitent King David.

p.76: Add. MS 30014, f.130v
Hymnal
1415
St Augustine surrounded by saints.

p.81: Add. MS 24098, f.27v
Book of Hours
Flanders, Bruges; c.1530; 115 x 80 mm
Simon Bening: calendar scene of everyday life for October.

p.82: (border, detail) Add. MS 18851, f.8v
The Isabella Breviary
Flanders, Bruges; end of the fifteenth century; 230 x 160 mm
Detail from decorative border surrounding a miniature of the twelve Sibyls foretelling the coming of Christ.

p.85: (detail) Burney MS 275, f.390v
Collection of scientific writings
France, Paris; c.1300; 410 x 290 mm
Animals with astronomical instruments; detail from decorative margin on the opening page of Ptolemy's *Almagest*.

p.86: Add. MS 36619, f.5
Ordinance of Charles the Bold
Flanders, possibly Brussels; c.1474–76; 305 x 216 mm
Army officers swearing allegiance to the Duke.

PUBLISHERS' ACKNOWLEDGMENTS

PROJECT EDITOR: Fiona Robertson
TEXT EDITOR: Cathy Herbert
PROOFREADER: Pat Farrington

ART EDITOR: Becky Clarke

PRODUCTION: Kim Oliver

The publishers would like to thank Kathleen Houghton and David Way at The British Library for their assistance with this book.